ABSOLUTE BEGINNERS
Piano

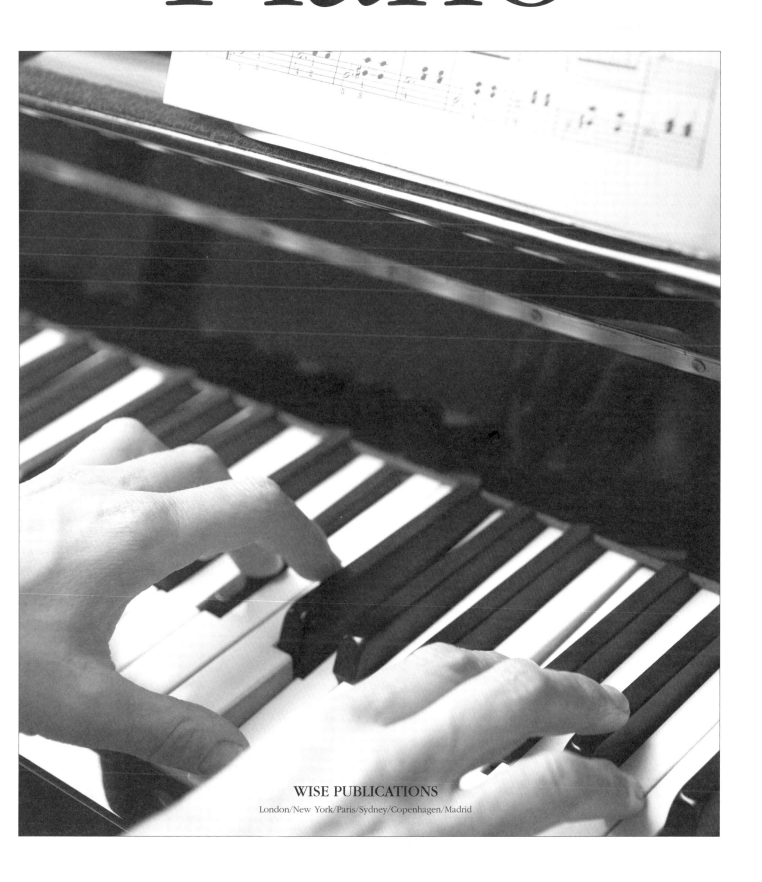

WISE PUBLICATIONS
London/New York/Paris/Sydney/Copenhagen/Madrid

GW00673740

Published by:
Music Sales Limited
14-15 Berners Street, London W1T 3LJ, UK.

Exclusive Distributors:
Music Sales Limited
Distribution Centre, Newmarket Road,
Bury St Edmunds, Suffolk IP33 3YB, UK.

Music Sales Corporation
257 Park Avenue South,
New York,
NY10010, USA.

Music Sales Pty Limited
120 Rothschild Avenue,
Rosebery, NSW 2018,
Australia.

Order No.AM986425
ISBN 1-84609-662-6

Printed in the EU.
CD recorded, mixed and mastered by John Rose and Jonas Persson.
Music processed by Paul Ewers.
Backing tracks by Guy Dagul.
Edited by Heather Slater.

Your Guarantee of Quality
As publishers, we strive to produce every book to the
highest commercial standards.

Particular care has been given to specifying acid-free,
neutral-sized paper made from pulps which have not
been elemental chlorine bleached. This pulp is from
farmed sustainable forests and was produced with
special regard for the environment.

Throughout, the printing and binding have been
planned to ensure a sturdy, attractive publication
which should give years of enjoyment. If your copy
fails to meet our high standards, please inform us and
we will gladly replace it.

www.musicsales.com

Contents

Introduction

Welcome to Absolute Beginners Piano.

This book will teach you all of the essential basics you need to know to play the piano, and will get you started playing—fast!

You'll start by playing short examples, and very soon you'll be playing whole pieces with both hands together.

The **easy-to-follow instructions** will guide you through:

- correct posture and playing position
- finding the notes on the piano keyboard
- reading basic music notation, learning note names and understanding rhythm
- playing with hands separately and together

Listen to the CD as you learn—the audio will let you hear how the music should sound—and then try to play the piano part with the backing tracks.

And always remember: practice makes perfect! It's best to practise a small amount often because you are teaching your muscles to memorise certain repeated actions—twenty minutes each day is far better than two hours at the weekend with nothing in between.

No matter what type of music you want to play—classical, jazz, popular—the basic techniques are all the same. Once you master them, you'll be well on your way to playing in whatever style you prefer.

A good playing position means that you'll be comfortable at the piano, and this will help you to play well.

Sit facing the middle of the piano keyboard with your feet right in front of the pedals, and try to keep your back reasonably straight. Avoid tension in any part of your body, particularly in your lower arms.

If you sit too high or too low, you'll find it more difficult to play accurately—and your arms will get tired very quickly!

Also make sure you are sitting a comfortable distance away from the keyboard—if you sit too far away, you'll find it hard to reach the upper and lower notes, and if you sit too close you'll be restricting your arm movement.

You will find it easier to play if you keep your fingernails quite short, so that the pads of your fingers, and not your fingernails, are making direct contact with the keys.

When playing the piano, wear something comfortable so that your arms can move freely.

Ideally, your seat should be at a height which allows your forearms to sit level with, or just above, the piano keyboard. An adjustable piano stool is preferable to an ordinary chair because it will allow for adjustments according to your height.

Make sure that you keep your wrists up and steady, and don't let your wrists drop to or below the level of the keyboard.

Correct   **Incorrect**

Fingering

Fingering is a system that assigns certain fingers to certain notes on the piano keyboard, and it's what keeps your fingers from getting tangled up in knots when you play!

This is how it works: each finger on each hand is given a number from 1 to 5, as shown in the photograph below. You will see these numbers over the notes in the music—they tell you which finger to use when you are playing a particular note.

Try to stick to the recommended fingerings for each piece and you'll soon get into the habit of having your hands in the correct position.

CHECKPOINT

WHAT YOU'VE ACHIEVED SO FAR...

You can now:

- Sit at the piano in the correct position
- Place your hands on the keyboard correctly
- Understand right and left hand fingerings

Left hand

Right hand

Tip

Try resting a small coin on the back of your hand as you place your hands on the piano keyboard. You should be able to play quite comfortably without the coin falling off!

Proper hand position involves not just your fingers, but your wrists. Your hand should be supported from the wrist, and it's very important that you don't let your wrist fall below keyboard level.

With your fingers sitting lightly above the keys, curl them slightly as if you're holding an imaginary ball.

Or, try this—place your relaxed hand on your knee so that it is covering your kneecap. Then, carefully lift your hand from your knee to the keyboard, and it will be in the proper, curved position.

Your fingertips should cover five adjacent notes in each hand, as in the photo below. This is the normal five-finger position, and this is how you should begin when you are playing the exercises in this book.

Finding your way around

At first glance, the piano keyboard may seem confusing—there are so many notes! But it is actually the same series of 12 notes repeated over and over again for the entire length of the keyboard. Only 7 letter names are used: C, D, E, F, G, A and B.

The black keys are arranged in two and threes in a repeating pattern—this pattern is very useful, because it helps you to find your way around the keyboard.

These are the notes you will learn in this book:

How the piano works

The word 'piano' is short for 'pianoforte', which is an Italian term meaning 'soft-loud'.

The piano was given this name because the volume of its sound is controlled by the force with which the keys are struck—in other words, a piano, unlike an electronic keyboard, can be played quietly or loudly, or at any volume in between.

There are many types of pianos, but they are all constructed in basically the same way. The inside of a piano looks a bit like a harp, with strings ranging in size from quite thick, for the low notes, to very thin, for the high notes.

The sound is produced when these strings are struck by small felt-covered 'hammers', which spring into action when you strike a key.

Reading music

Reading music is really quite easy once you understand the fundamentals.

A musical note has just two properties: **pitch** and **duration**. Pitch tells you how high or low a note is—low is to the left on the keyboard, and high is to the right—and duration tells you how long the note should last and when it is to be played in relation to the other notes.

The five lines on which the notes are placed are called a **stave**. A note placed on the top of the stave will sound higher than a note placed on the bottom.

For piano players there is one stave for the right hand and one for the left hand. For the first part of this book we'll be using only the right hand.

Jargon Buster

Duration – how long a note lasts
Pitch – how high or low a note is
Stave – the five lines on which music is written

Music has a basic **rhythm**, or **pulse**—when you tap your foot to a song, you are responding to the rhythm of the music.

Rhythm is created when multiples of **beats** are grouped together into larger units called **bars**, or **measures**. This pattern of beat determines the rhythm of a piece of music.

To get used to counting 'in time', try this exercise— count steadily from 1 to 4 and then repeat the sequence a few times, like this:

1 - 2 - 3 - 4 / 1 - 2 - 3 - 4 / 1 - 2 - 3 - 4 / repeat...

Each time you count '1' you are at the beginning of a new bar. It's that simple!

Note values

If you look at a piece of music you'll see that notes have different shapes—some have tails, some have solid note heads, while others are hollow. Each type of note lasts for a different number of beats.

Time signatures

At the beginning of every piece of music, you will see a **time signature**. The most common time signature is 4/4, which looks like this:

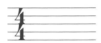

A time signature tells you how many notes of what value to play in each bar. The bottom number represents the note value, and the top number represents the number of those notes that will fit into each bar. So in **4/4 time**, there are 4 crotchets (i.e. 'quarter' notes) per bar.

Tip

4/4 time is sometimes called **common time**, with a time signature that looks like this:

𝄴

A note that looks like this **o** is called a **semibreve**. A semibreve lasts for the duration of a full bar—in other words, it has a count of four beats. You would count a semibreve like this:

This note 𝅗𝅥 is called a **minim**, and it lasts for two beats. A minim is counted like this:

This note ♩ is called a **crotchet**, and it lasts for one beat. There are four of these to every bar and they are counted like this:

You can put any combination of these notes in a bar as long as they add up to four. So, as you can see, rhythm is quite a bit like basic maths! You now know enough about rhythm to play some music.

Your first note

Let's find your first note: **Middle C**.

Middle C is a white key, and the easiest way to locate a white key is to see where it fits into the pattern of black keys.

Look for the groups of two black keys, and then find the note right in the middle—you have just found the note D. C is directly to the left of D, or to the left of the group of two black keys.

You'll notice that the groups of black keys are repeated all the way up the piano keyboard, so there are many different Cs. In order to distinguish between them we usually refer to one of them as middle C, which is, just as you would expect, the one closest to the centre of the piano keyboard.

Locate middle C on your piano—on most pianos, it is the closest C to the manufacturer's label.

Now try to play a few different Cs. The diagram below shows you how to find the C below middle C and the C above middle C.

Jargon Buster

A **leger line** is a tiny horizontal line placed just above or below the stave, which allows us to write notes which are higher or lower than the stave. Middle C is an example of a note that is written on a leger line.

This is what middle C looks like on the stave:

Notice that middle C is written on a small line directly under the main stave. This is called a leger line, and it allows us to write notes that are higher or lower than the stave's five lines and four spaces. It is important that you can tell one C from another, or else you might play the right notes (according to their name) but in the wrong place on the keyboard!

The examples on the next few pages all use middle C and the notes just above it.

Now you're ready to play your first piece.

Don't worry about reading music—as long as you can count to four and you can remember where C is, then you can play this piece!

Using the CD

The CD in the back of this book will help you. On track 1, you will hear the piece below played with a backing track.

On track 2, you will hear just the backing track so you can try it yourself.

After the four-beat intro click, play a C for four beats with the accompanying music, then rest for four beats, then play for four and rest for four, and so on until the end of the piece.

The symbol ▬ is called a rest, and it is there to tell you when not to play. You'll learn more about rests a bit further on in this book.

The piece lasts for eight bars. This means that you'll be counting to four 8 times in a row. This may seem simple, but already you're teaching yourself the important discipline of playing in time.

Remember!

Keep your arms parallel to the keys and your fingers curved when you are playing.

Learning to count regular beats is something that you will eventually do automatically. But for now, it will help to count out loud while you are playing.

Track 1 on the CD demonstrates how this piece should sound, and **Track 2** gives you a backing track that you can play along with.

Count: 1 2 3 4   1 2 3 4   1 2 3 4   1 2 3 4   etc.

New notes D and E

Now you're ready to learn two more notes—but first, take a moment to review the pattern of keys on the keyboard, as shown below:

Here is the note D, which you first found in between the groups of 2 black notes. Make sure you are playing the one directly to the right of middle C.

D

Just to the right of D is the note E:

E

Now you know three notes—play every group of C-D-E that you can find on the keyboard, naming them out loud as you go.

Below is a tune that will help you remember these notes. Always play C with the thumb of your right hand (1), D with your index finger (2), and E with your middle finger (3). Say the names of the notes as you play them, and allow four beats (or one bar) per note.

Watch out for the one bar of rest after each group of three notes. The beat numbers are written over the music to help you count.

Keep your hand in a relaxed position, avoiding tension in your shoulders, lower arms and hands. Press each note firmly and play smoothly, or **legato.**

Jargon Buster

Legato (Italian for 'smoothly') is a term used to describe the way in which successive notes are played on the piano. To play legato, you hold each note just until you have played the next one—you should release the first note at the exact moment you strike the second one. This will ensure that one note does not overlap with the next, and that there are no 'gaps' between notes.

The opposite of legato is **staccato** ('detached'), which means that the notes are not joined together, but are shortened instead so that there are gaps between notes. In this book, you will only be playing legato, so be aware of this concept of playing smoothly, with no gaps.

Keep the tempo slow to start with, gradually increasing speed as you become more confident.

Listen to the demonstration on **Track 3** and then play along with the backing track on **Track 4**.

New notes F, G, A and B

B

Remember, you can use the pattern of the black notes to help you find the white ones. Look at the diagram below, and notice the repeating pattern of three black keys.

Reading from left to right, the notes you've just learned are **F**, **G**, **A** and **B**. Practise finding each note and say the letter names out loud as you play.

Tip

If you're having trouble memorising the names and locations of all the notes, try placing labelled stickers onto the keys.

Playing F to B and a new C

Now that you know how to count beats and bars, let's try an exercise that will familiarise you with your new notes.

This exercise will also let you count in a new way, as each note has two beats instead of one (in other words, you will be playing minims instead of crotchets).

For this exercise play the lower note (F) with the thumb of your right hand, keeping the relaxed hand position you learned earlier. Keep your other fingers 'hovering' over the other notes.

Listen to the demonstration on **Track 5** and then play along with the backing track on **Track 6**.

A new note in the right hand

So far, you have learned to play seven notes, from middle C up to B. The note to the right of B is another C—this note is one **octave**, or eight notes, higher than middle C.

Jargon Buster

An **interval** is the distance between any two notes on the keyboard.

An **octave** is an interval of eight notes—in other words, two notes that are one octave apart have exactly eight notes separating them. Notes that are an octave apart will always have the same name, so the note that is an octave away from C is C, the note that is an octave away from F is F, and so on.

Octave

The same five lines (the stave) that we use for music played by the right hand are also used for music played by the left hand. To indicate which notes are to be played by which hand, we use a **clef**.

For the right hand we use a **treble clef**:

For the left hand we use a **bass clef**:

You'll notice that these clefs are each anchored on the stave at a specific point, and this can help you to identify the notes.

The treble clef curls around the second line of the staff (from bottom to top), which is the note G:

The bass clef is anchored around the note F:

In the example above, notice that the two dots to the right of the bass clef are at either side of the line upon which the note F sits.

Using these clues—the treble clef curls around G and the bass clef's dots surround F—you can work out the position of every note on the stave, for both the right and left hand.

Jargon Buster

A **clef** (French for 'key') is the symbol that appears at the beginning of every piece of music. The **treble clef** is used for right-hand notes—the **bass clef** is used for left-hand notes.

B C D E F G A B middle C D E F G A B C D E

CHECKPOINT

WHAT YOU'VE ACHIEVED SO FAR...

You can now:
• Play eight notes
• Understand basic concepts of pitch and rhythm
• Read music from the stave

Left-hand notes

Here are your first notes in the bass clef, to be played with your left hand.

C

D

E

F

G

C D E F G

Tip

From now on, the diagrams will show all the notes on both staves, with treble and bass clefs. Review pages 16-19 if you are unsure of the location of the notes on the staves.

Playing notes and rests

Here's an exercise designed to get you used to playing with your left hand.

Remember this symbol ━? It's called a **rest,** and in this piece every one of these rests has the same value as a semibreve. In other words, each rest indicates that you are not to play for four beats.

Count the rests even though you're not playing—that way you will always stay in time.

Listen to the demonstration on **Track** 7 and then play along with the backing track on **Track 8**.

Tip

Remember that the finger numbers start at 1 with the thumb, going down to 5 for the little finger.

ABSOLUTE BEGINNERS
Piano Guide

The Piano Keyboard

There are only seven letter names used in music:

A B C D E F G

These seven letter names repeat over and
over again on the piano keyboard. The black keys
are arranged in groups of twos and threes.

How To Learn The White Keys: C, D & E

Use the black keys to locate the white keys.
For example, 'D' lies between two black keys.

To the left of D lies C. To the right of D lies E.

How To Learn The White Keys: F, G, A & B

Use the groups of three black keys to locate F, G, A & B
(the remaining four letters of the musical alphabet):

Find all the Fs, Gs, As & Bs on your piano. Play each
note in turn and name it as you play.

You now know all the white notes and their names.

An Important Note: Middle C

One of the most important notes on the piano
is middle C. This is the C nearest the middle of
the instrument, directly opposite the manufacturer's
name, as you sit at the piano.

Look at the illustration above.

You will see three Cs:

The C below middle C
Middle C
The C above middle C

Try to locate these Cs on your piano keyboard.

Here is an easy way to learn how to find them:

• Play middle C with the right hand (any finger).
• Play middle C with the left hand.
• Play the C below middle C with the left hand.
• Play the C above middle C with the right hand.
• Finally: play middle C again with one of the
  fingers of each hand.

You now know how to find middle C and
the Cs immediately above and below it.

Sitting Correctly

It is important to sit correctly at the piano.
The more comfortable you are, the easier it
will be to play well.

Sit facing the middle of the instrument, with
your feet right in front of the pedals. Sit upright,
keeping your back as straight as possible but not rigid.
Your seat should be high enough to allow your arms
to be level with the keyboard, and you should sit far
enough away that your arms have full range of
movement.

Hand Position

Support your hands from the wrists, which should
be in a steady position. If you move your wrists
too much as you play, you will soon experience
muscle fatigue.

Curve your fingers as if you are gently holding
an imaginary ball. Don't extend your fingers
into the keys; instead, allow the natural position
of your hand to determine which part of the key
you depress with the tip of your finger.

Five-Finger Playing Position

With the tips of your fingers, cover five adjacent
white notes in each hand. This is the normal
five-finger playing position.

Always return to this position when you have
been playing on other parts of the keyboard.
Like a good squash or tennis player always
occupying the centre of the court, this is the
best 'alert' position for piano players.

So far, everything you have played has been in stepwise motion—that is, the notes sit right beside each other on the keyboard. Now you will play a piece in which the notes are several steps apart. Bass lines often move this way, so it's important that you train your left hand to play these patterns.

If you concentrate on keeping your hand in the right position and follow the fingering numbers, you'll soon get it.

Listen to the demonstration on **Track 9** and then play along with the backing track on **Track 10**.

Count: 1 2 3 4   1 2 3 4   1 2 3 4   1 2 3 4 etc.

Intervals in the left hand

In this exercise, your left hand is moving over a distance, or **interval**, of four notes (from C to F, and then from D to G). An interval of four notes is called a **fourth**, because there are four notes separating the top note from the bottom note.

Similarly, when the top and bottom notes are five notes apart, this interval is called a **fifth**. Bass lines often move in intervals of fourths and fifths.

CHECKPOINT

WHAT YOU'VE ACHIEVED SO FAR...

You can now:
- Count and read different rhythms
- Read music in the treble and bass clefs
- Use both your left and right hands

Hands together, ties and rests

Now you are ready to play with both hands at the same time.

Take a close look at the exercise at the top of the next page before you play. Notice that, in the last bar of the piece, you only play for one beat—the remainder of the bar is filled with rests.

Also notice the curved lines joining the notes in the last bar to the notes in the second-last bar. They are called ties, and they simply add the value of one note to the other.

For example, if a semibreve (4 beats) is tied to a minim (2 beats), you hold it for a total of 6 beats:

Count: 1   2   3   4   1   2   3   4

Look at the last two bars of the exercise on the next page. With your left hand, you'll play a C semibreve in the second-last bar—then, instead of restriking the C in the last bar, you will hold the semibreve you just played for one extra beat (as indicated by the tie, which leads to a crotchet).

So the last C in the left hand lasts for 5 beats (4+1), and the E in the right hand lasts for three beats (2+1).

Take your time with this exercise, and make sure you are confident with your counting and with the movement of your left hand before moving on.

Now that you are familiar with the note names, you'll no longer see them written directly below the music.

Listen to the demonstration on **Track 11** and then play along with the backing track on **Track 12**.

▼ Here's where your hands should be, ready to start playing.

About rests

Rests tell us when not to play, and they have the same rhythmic values as their corresponding notes. You've already played pieces that contain rests, but let's take a closer look at the different types of rests.

A rest for a semibreve lasts for four beats, and looks like this:

A rest for a minim lasts for two beats, and looks like this:

A crotchet rest lasts for one beat, and looks like this:

Just like different notes, you can combine different rests. For example, for a silence of three beats, you could combine a minim rest (2 beats) with a crotchet rest (1 beat), like this:

New notes and review

Well done! You now know eight notes in the right hand and five notes in the left hand. Take a moment to review the notes you know.

To review, play through all of your notes very slowly, reminding yourself of the note name and its relation to the stave and the keyboard.

Right-hand review

C D E F G A B C

Left-hand review

C D E F G

Your last two new notes!

To play the rest of the music in this book, you need to learn just two more notes: A in the left hand and B in the right hand.

These notes are usually played with the thumbs, as in the diagram below. Now you can play two octaves, from the C below middle C to the C above.

Chords

When you play more than one note simultaneously, this is called a **chord**. You can play a chord with the left hand or the right hand, or with both hands at the same time. There are many different types of chords, but here are a few that you can master in seconds.

C major

F major

G major

In this book, you'll be playing chords in which most of the notes are played by the right hand. Eventually you will be able to add more and more notes to these chords and involve the left hand as well.

The next piece of music features chords. Before you try this piece, look carefully at the fingerings, as they differ slightly from the standard chord fingerings you have just learned.

This is because, when you are moving from one chord to another, you need to prepare the hand so that the transition from one chord to the next is smooth.

Take a look at the first two bars. To move smoothly to the second chord, which is played with fingers 1, 3 and 5, you need to prepare by playing the first chord with fingers 1, 2 and 4. When the first chord comes back again in bar 5 you can use the standard 1-3-5 fingering because this will help you get to the chord in bar 6, which is played with fingers 1, 2 and 5.

Concentrate on mastering these fingerings, as they will help you to play even the most complicated chord progressions with ease!

Listen to the demonstration on **Track 13** and then play along with the backing track on **Track 14**.

Chords with both hands

Now let's add the left hand. The left and right hands share the job of playing the notes that make up a chord. The left hand often plays fewer notes than the right hand, and they are more widely spaced.

Practise the exercise on the next page one hand at a time. You already know the right hand part, as it's exactly the same as in the previous exercise, but now you will be adding single notes in the left hand.

Remember: when you are playing chords, hand and finger position are especially important. From the one basic hand position you have been using so far, you should be able to play this exercise without moving your hands away from the keys.

Tip

Make sure you play all of the notes in each chord at precisely the same time, and listen carefully to ensure that all of the notes are sounding at the same volume.

Also, concentrate on keeping your hands in a steady position while you are playing—you should always aim to avoid any unnecessary hand movements.

C major

F major

G major

Now play the exercise below, and remember to watch your fingering—try to move as smoothly as possible from one chord to the next.

Listen to the demonstration on **Track 15** and then play along with the backing track on **Track 16**.

Count: I 2 3 4   I 2 3 4   I 2 3 4   I 2 3 4 etc

Moving the right hand

In this exercise, your right hand moves between G and A while the left hand remains steady.

Remember that the crotchets in the right hand have a count of one beat each, while the semibreves in the left hand have a count of four beats each.

Watch out for the sudden stop at the end, where you only play on the first beat of the bar and then rest.

Listen to the demonstration on **Track 17** and then play along with the backing track on **Track 18**.

Here's an exercise for moving your left hand while keeping your right hand in place. The left hand is moving every two beats—be careful to keep the lower note (a C) constant while you move to the A with your thumb.

Also, notice that in the last bar you play for two beats and then rest for two beats.

Listen to the demonstration on **Track 19** and then play along with the backing track on **Track 20**.

Quavers and repeat signs

You've already played crotchets, minims and semibreves—now you'll learn about a new note-value, the **quaver**. A quaver lasts for just one half of one beat. In other words, a quaver is the equivalent of one half of a crotchet.

In a 4/4 bar, quavers are counted like this:

An easy way to remember the duration of a crotchet compared to a quaver is to call a crotchet 'tea' and two quavers 'coffee'. Look at the example below and say the words under the stave rhythmically:

Here is a tune full of crotchets and quavers.

Before you play, speak the words in time. Then play at a slow tempo and count with a steady beat so you can focus on accuracy. Practise it a few times slowly until you can speed up and still be accurate.

Notice the symbol :‖ at the end of the piece. This is called a **repeat sign**. This means that you need to go back to the beginning and play the whole piece one more time.

Listen to the demonstration on **Track 21** and then play along with the backing track on **Track 22**.

You will often see a small dot just to the right of a note. This dot is similar to a tie, in that it extends the duration of a note. A dotted note is held for an additional half of its original value—so a dotted crotchet would be held for a beat and a half. Clap this rhythm while counting out loud:

Jargon Buster

The term **dotted note** refers to a note that has a small dot just to its right. This dot extends the duration of the note by one-half of its original value.

Now, keep counting but clap only the notes shown below:

Now play the example below, counting carefully so that the quavers fall in exactly the right place.

Listen to **Track 23** for a demonstration of the exercise below and play along for practice.

Here in an excerpt from Franz Schubert's Symphony No.9, which has dotted notes in the right hand.

Listen to the demonstration on **Track 24** and then play along with the backing track on **Track 25**.

Waltz rhythm (3/4)

So far, all of the music you have played has been in 4/4 time—in other words, you have been playing 4 crotchet beats per bar. Another common grouping of beats is 3/4, which means that there are 3 crotchet beats in each bar. This is sometimes called 'waltz rhythm'—hum a few bars of a waltz, and you'll know exactly what 3/4 time feels like!

Or, try this—count steadily to 3 and keep repeating, and emphasise the '1' each time you say it to get the feel of waltz rhythm:

1 - 2 - 3 / 1 - 2 - 3 / 1 - 2 - 3 etc.

When you are playing in 3/4 time you will often encounter this note ♩. This is a dotted minim, and it lasts for 3 beats.

You'll remember that a dot to the right of a note extends the note's duration by one-half—so a dotted minim is worth its original 2 beats plus one more (a crotchet) to equal 3:

The piece below is in 3/4 time. Count a few bars in your head before starting to play, and practise slowly until you are confident with 3/4 time.

Listen to the demonstration on **Track 26** and then play along with the backing track on **Track 27**.

Before playing the complete pieces on the next five pages, take a moment to review the notes you've learned. Make sure you are familiar with each note's location on the keyboard and position on the stave.

Jingle Bells *Traditional*

Now you're ready to play your first complete song. Before you play, take a look at the time signature, starting hand position, and suggested fingerings.

You'll notice that there is very little movement in the left hand, so just keep that hand very steady, and focus on the right-hand melody.

Listen to the demonstration on **Track 28** and then play along with the backing track on **Track 29**.

Drink To Me Only *Traditional*

Here is another song in 3/4 time. Remember to place a slight emphasis on the first beat of each bar so that you really feel the waltz rhythm.

In this piece, you will see some new instructions: **Fine** and **D.C. al Fine**. This means that a section of the piece is to be repeated.

Once you have reached the end, the words 'D.C. al Fine' tell you to start again at the beginning, and stop when you reach the word 'Fine,' or 'end'.

Listen to the demonstration on **Track 30** and then play along with the backing track on **Track 31**.

Here is a piece that uses mainly crotchets, but there are some quaver patterns that you may find tricky at first.

Take a look at the right-hand notes in bar 8, where you play a dotted crotchet followed by a quaver and then four quavers in a row. Practise this very slowly and hands separately at first.

Also notice that, in bar 12, the melody switches from right to left hand. Follow the fingering suggested and make sure that you let go of the right-hand D before you play the left-hand G.

Listen to the demonstration on **Track 32** and then play along with the backing track on **Track 33**.

Largo from 'New World' Symphony *Antonín Dvořák*

Here are those dotted crotchets again!

Count steadily, and when you play a dotted crotchet make sure that the quaver that follows it comes in precisely on the second half of the beat.

As in 'Drink To Me Only', you will need to repeat the first section of this piece as indicated by the **Fine** and **D.C. al Fine** signs.

Listen to the demonstration on **Track 34** and then play along with the backing track on **Track 35**.

Lullaby *Johannes Brahms*

Here is a piece of music that presents a new challenge. Although you know all of the notes, you will be moving away slightly from your usual hand position, so you'll need to pay close attention to your fingering. Notice that although you start on E, you begin with your thumb instead of finger 3.

Follow the suggested fingerings carefully so that your hand stays in the correct position.

Listen to the demonstration on **Track 36** and then play along with the backing track on **Track 37**.

WELL DONE!

You now know the basics of playing the piano and reading music, and are well on your way to becoming a proficient pianist. Keep practising the pieces and the concepts you have learned in this book and soon you'll be able to get around the piano keyboard with confidence.

THIS IS WHAT YOU'VE ACHIEVED...

You can now:

- Sit comfortably at the keyboard, and play with the correct hand and finger position
- Find 6 left-hand and 9 right-hand notes on the piano
- Read basic note values and pitches
- Read from both the treble and bass clefs
- Play right and left hand chords
- Play left and right hands together